The Camping
Cookbook

The Camping
Cookbook

First published in 2011
LOVE FOOD is an imprint of Parragon Books Ltd

Parragon
Queen Street House
4 Queen Street
Bath BA1 1HE, UK

ISBN: 978-4454-2870-3

Printed in China

Photography by Mike Cooper
Insert photography by Jim Johnston
Home economy by Lincoln Jefferson
Additional photography by Sian Irvine
Additional home economy by Katie Giovanni
Text and additional recipes by Rachel Carter

Special thanks to Ben, Benedict, Lucy, and Polly.

Notes for the Reader

This book uses imperial, metric, and US cup measurements. Follow the same units of measurement throughout; do not mix imperial and metric. All spoon measurements are level: teaspoons are assumed to be 5 ml, and tablespoons are assumed to be 15 ml. Unless otherwise stated, milk is assumed to be whole, eggs and individual vegetables such as potatoes are medium, and pepper is freshly ground black pepper.

The times given are an approximate guide only. Preparation times differ according to the techniques used by different people and the cooking times may also vary from those given as a result of the type of oven used. Optional ingredients, variations, or serving suggestions have not been included in the calculations.

Recipes using raw or very lightly cooked eggs should be avoided by infants, the elderly, pregnant women, convalescents, and anyone with a chronic condition. Pregnant and breast-feeding women are advised to avoid eating peanuts and peanut products. People with nut allergies should be aware that some of the prepared ingredients used in the recipes in this book may contain nuts. Always check the packaging before use.

Picture acknowledgments

The publisher would like to thank the following for permission to reproduce copyright material on page 10-11: Smores!©Gena Hayward/Getty Images and page 168: Banana on barbecue grill rack, close up©Foodcollection/Getty Images

Contents

Getting Started

Camping doesn't mean you have to be a backpacker, carrying everything with you into the wilderness. Modern camping captures the idealistic notion of enjoying nature and getting away from the busy pace of modern life. Troubles seem forgotten and worries disappear as you settle into a way of living that you can never really create elsewhere. Living under canvas is a lot of fun—you quickly realize that you can live without the television, the Internet, and all the modern conveniences that are part of daily life. Stripped back to the basics, everyday living is really simple.

When buying your camping equipment, you don't need every gadget available—start with the basics and wait to see whether you enjoy it first. Whatever your budget, you'll find something to suit you, either in department stores and specialty outdoor stores or online.

The tent will naturally be your biggest purchase. If you are planning longer trips away choose one large enough to stand up in and eat in if the weather is bad. If your budget allows, buy bigger than you need—that extra space will prove invaluable to store things in!

Other important equipment will be the bedding (air mattress, sleeping bag, or both) and your cooking utensils. Large plastic storage containers are ideal for utensils and means you're ready to go, whenever the urge to camp strikes you. Finally, a good set of collapsible chairs and a table that won't collapse while you're eating your meal are an investment worth making.

There are plenty of good camp stoves available, but the size of your stove will depend on how many people you are cooking for and how complex the meals will be. For simple meals for 1 or 2 people, a single-burner stove will be sufficient. For feeding larger groups, the larger multiburner options would be more suitable. Other useful points to consider are, the easiness of setting up the stove, and the lightness of the equipment (if you have to carry it a distance from the car to the campsite). You should choose the smallest, lightest stove to suit your needs.

Try planning a few meals before you go, and make sure you discuss food ideas with everyone who's involved in the camping trip (which will save a lot of arguing later on). Then all the meals can be arranged in advance so all that's required are a few essential ingredients and maybe some fresh and frozen items taken from home. All that's left is to cook, eat, and enjoy!

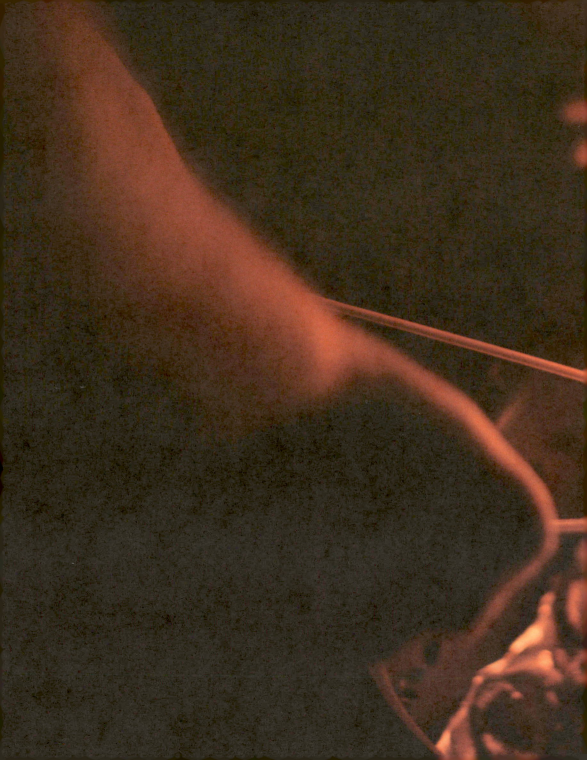

Equipment & Ingredient List

cheese grater

dish soap

dish towel

paper towels

sponge

salt and pepper

spoons, forks, and knives

wooden spoons

aluminum foil

plastic wrap

wax paper

sharp knife

corkscrew

cutting board

shallow frying pan

frying pan with lid

mugs

vegetable cutting board

tongs

heat resistant bowls

pocket knife

potato masher

wooden skewers

eggcups

meat cutting board

chopping knife

serving bowls

plates

pans

medium saucepan

small saucepan

large nonstick frying pan

cooler

Hints & Tips For Setting up your Tent

Before you arrive at your campsite, it's worth having a test run with your tent in the backyard. If it proves difficult, then take some photos of the tent as it goes up and keep with the instructions. Color coding poles can also be helpful.

When you get to your campsite, choosing your campsite carefully is important. Try to avoid anywhere that looks wet and muddy. It's also important to look for shelter from the wind and sun and try to avoid setting up next to any facilities. Do a complete check for animal waste before setting on a location—whether it's the wild animal or dog variety, you don't want it walked through your tent!

A level patch of ground is preferable, and check that there are no sharp stones or tree roots in the vicinity that might poke through your tent and tear a hole. An extra tarp can be useful to put down, because it will protect the tent from damage.

Buy some spare tent stakes to take with you. In addition, an extra hammer can be useful, especially if your tent is large, because it will allow two people to set up the tent to help speed up the process.

Campsite Cooking

cooking with gas

The simplest way of cooking is on a basic propane or gas camping stove. These start with a basic one-burner version, which uses a small gas canister and is ideal for boiling a pot of water or perhaps heating a can of beans in a saucepan.

For a little more versatility, try a small camp stove. These are collapsible, often supplied in a handy carrying case and with either two or three burners and usually a small grill and wind protection around the sides. This size is suitable for a wide variety of meals and most of the recipes in this book.

If you're getting serious about camping and you're away for more than a weekend then you may want to invest in more specialized equipment, including a camping oven for baking, which gets its heat from a two- to three-burner camp stove.

cooking on the barbecue

At a very basic level, disposable barbecues are so inexpensive that they are perfect for a night or two away if you don't want the hassle of getting an authentic barbecue started. These are ideal for cooking a small breakfast or dinner. You can now buy a custom-made stand to hold these mini barbecues above the ground, which prevents the grass from scorching. Inspired by Argentinian cowboys, the "Asado" stand is a cool and stylish addition to your camping equipment.

If you want to use charcoal to start your own barbecue, there are plenty of reasonably priced portable barbecues or grills that can be quickly assembled. These are cheap to buy, with folding legs

for easy storage and are ideal for cooking a range of foods, such as burgers, steaks, or fish, whether it's on the campsite or the beach. They heat up quickly and retain heat, making them small but wonderfully efficient.

If you want to spend a little more, gas-powered barbecues are extremely efficient as well as being easy to use and clean. They have the added benefit of providing instant heat if you need to eat in a hurry. At the top end of the market are very sophisticated models with interchangeable cooking surfaces, a stove, and a reversible nonstick grill, among other features. These models are immensely versatile and portable and are ideal when cooking for larger numbers of people. Whatever your needs and choice, try and buy from a reputable dealer where you should be guaranteed a quality appliance that will last.

cooking over the campfire

Cooking over the campfire is perhaps the most idealistic vision of cooking outdoors. It is hard to beat the taste of food cooked over a campfire, especially if you add some flavored woodchips to give your food a hickory taste (instructions on how to use the woodchips can be found on the back of their packaging). And marshmallows popped on the end of a stick and toasted over the campfire as night falls will always delight, no matter what your age.

Campfire cooking requires a clean-burning, hot fire. This is only achieved with dry, seasoned wood—if the wood is damp, your fire will be smoky and will not burn correctly. The same thing goes for any sign of a medium–strong wind—unless you are well sheltered, this is one battle you will not win. If conditions are favorable, a camping grill rack placed over the fire will cook your food to perfection. This method of cooking requires constant attention to ensure that the food doesn't catch on fire, and be sure to wait until the fire is beginning to die off before you start cooking, otherwise the heat will be too strong.

"Don't Forget" Check List

- Toilet paper
- Plastic garbage bags
- resealable bags
- Waterproof matches
- Headlamp
- Antibacterial wipes
- Hand soap
- Clothespins and clothes line
- Pocket mirror
- Flashlight (wind-up type is best)
- First-aid kit
- Radio
- Water carrier
- Sun cream
- Mosquito repellent
- Insulated lunch bag
- Can/bottle opener

Cooking Essentials

Prepare these recipes before you head off and you'll have plenty of lunch and dinner ideas for your camping trip, with minimum fuss.

Heat the tomato sauce and add as a topping to baked potatoes with plenty of grated cheese

Slice open a bagel, toast on the campfire, spread with the tomato sauce, and add thick wedges of cheese for a heart-warming lunch

fresh tomato sauce

Stir through pasta, and add some cooked ground beef and chopped onions for a speedy Spaghetti with meat sauce

Heat the sauce through and add some chopped sausages, cooked on the campfire.

makes about 4 cups
1 tbsp olive oil
1 small onion, chopped
2–3 garlic cloves, crushed (optional)
1 small celery stalk, finely chopped
1 bay leaf
1 lb/450 g ripe tomatoes, peeled and chopped
1 tbsp tomato paste, blended with ⅔ cup water
pepper
few sprigs fresh oregano

Heat the oil in a heavy-bottom pan, add the onion, garlic, if using, celery, and bay leaf, and gently sauté, stirring frequently, for 5 minutes.

Stir in the tomatoes with the blended tomato paste. Add pepper to taste and the oregano. Bring to a boil, then reduce the heat, cover, and simmer, stirring occasionally, for 20–25 minutes, until the tomatoes have completely collapsed. If liked, simmer for an additional 20 minutes to produce a thicker sauce.

Discard the bay leaf and the oregano. Transfer to a food processor and process to a chunky paste. If a smooth sauce is preferred, pass through a fine nonmetallic strainer. Taste and adjust the seasoning, if necessary. Reheat and use as required.

Stir through pasta, add some Parmesan shavings, and enjoy

Add to mashed potatoes for a s-mashing side dish

Serve with a can of tuna and add as a topping to baked potato

basil pesto

Stir through freshly-boiled potatoes and top with trusty Parmesan

Slice open a roll, toast on the campfire, spread with pesto, and add some cream cheese and sun-dried tomatoes for a yummy lunch

makes about 1 cup
1⅓ cups fresh basil leaves
1 garlic clove
¼ cup toasted pine nuts
½–⅔ cup extra virgin olive oil
¼ cup freshly grated Parmesan cheese
1–2 tsp freshly squeezed lemon juice (optional)
salt and pepper

Tear the basil leaves and put in a large mortar with the garlic, pine nuts, and 1 tablespoon of the oil. Pound with a pestle to form a paste.

Gradually work in the remaining oil to form a thick sauce. Add salt and pepper to taste and stir in the Parmesan cheese. If liked, slacken slightly with the lemon juice.

Right Start Breakfast

Bacon Sandwiches

Serves 1

4 smoked bacon slices

1 tbsp olive oil

1 tbsp butter, softened

2 slices thick white or whole
wheat bread

1 tomato, sliced (optional)

condiment of choice,
such as ketchup or mustard

pepper

Cut the bacon in half. Add the oil to a nonstick frying pan and cook the bacon over a campfire, stove, or barbecue until cooked to your liking.

Meanwhile, butter the bread. Place 2 pieces of bacon on one slice of bread and season with a grinding of pepper. Add the tomato, if using, and the condiment.

Top with the remaining bacon and the other slice of bread and eat immediately. A serious contender for the best breakfast ever.

Breakfast Bagels

Serves 4

4 large portobello mushrooms

½ tbsp olive oil

4 eggs

4 bagels, halved and toasted

salt and pepper

Remove the entire stalk from the mushrooms. Cut out a small hollow from below each stalk, using the tip of a small sharp knife, to make room for the egg.

Place the oil in a nonstick frying pan and warm over a campfire, stove, or barbecue. Add the mushrooms 2 at a time with the hollowed side facing up. Cook gently for 4–5 minutes, turning once, until they start to soften.

Crack an egg into the hollow of each mushroom, season, and cook for an additional 6–8 minutes or until the eggs are cooked to your liking. Repeat with the remaining mushrooms.

Serve the egg-filled mushrooms on the toasted bagels.

English Muffins with Honey-Glazed Bacon & Eggs

Serves 2

1 tbsp olive oil

6 rindless unsmoked bacon slices

1 tbsp honey

3 oz/85 g canned corn kernels, drained

2 small tomatoes, diced

1 tbsp chopped fresh parsley

4 eggs

2 English muffins, split, toasted, and buttered

salt and pepper

Place the oil in a nonstick frying pan and warm over a campfire, stove, or barbecue. Lay the bacon slices in the frying pan and cook until lightly browned, then turn and cook the other side.

Warm the honey slightly and brush each bacon slice lightly with it. Cook the bacon for an additional 1 minute or so until it takes on a slight glaze. Remove from the frying pan and keep warm.

Mix the corn, diced tomatoes, and chopped parsley together and season to taste with salt and pepper. Fry, poach, or scramble the eggs, as you prefer.

Serve the honey-glazed bacon and eggs on buttered, toasted English muffins, topped with a spoonful of the corn-and-tomato mixture.

Why Skipping Breakfast Is Bad For You

Tempting though it may be to bounce out of your air bed in the morning and get straight into the next activity, it is well documented that missing breakfast is a big mistake. Here are some reasons why you shouldn't skip the first meal of the day:

Sharing a fully cooked breakfast or just a bacon sandwich with your friends and family is a great bonding experience (and the smell of bacon will drive your neighbors mad!).

If you're suffering from a camping hangover, then a good well-balanced breakfast will help you feel better.

It's a great opportunity to eat well and discuss the plans for the day ahead.

Set your children a good example. Eating breakfast is known to help concentration levels, and when they're back at school it's a good routine to keep to.

Eating first thing will put you in a better mood for the day ahead. Remember, you're on vacation—you will have a good time!

Breakfast in the outdoors on a campsite is an education in itself. We guarantee that the sights and sounds of other campers waking up and going about their everyday chores will be enough to make you appreciate the simple things in life.

It's potentially the best meal of the day. Bacon and eggs—need we say more?

Apple & Spice Porridge

Serves 4

2½ cups milk or water

1 tsp salt

1⅓ cups rolled oats

2 large apples

½ tsp ground allspice

honey (optional), to serve

Put the milk in a pan and bring to a boil over a campfire, stove, or barbecue. Add the salt and sprinkle in the oats, stirring constantly.

Place over low heat and let the oats simmer for 10 minutes, stirring occasionally.

Meanwhile, halve, core, and grate the apples. When the porridge is creamy and much of the liquid has evaporated, stir in the grated apple and allspice. Spoon into bowls and drizzle with the honey, if using.

Greek Yogurt with Honey, Nuts & Blueberries

Serves 4

3 tbsp honey

scant ¾ cup mixed
unsalted nuts

½ cup Greek yogurt

1 cup fresh blueberries

Gently heat the honey in a small pan over a campfire, stove,
or barbecue, add the nuts, and stir until they are well coated.
Remove from the heat and let cool slightly.

Divide the yogurt among 4 serving bowls, then spoon over the nut
mixture and blueberries.

Spicy Fried Eggs

Serves 2

2 tbsp olive oil

1 large onion, finely chopped

2 green or red bell peppers,
seeded and coarsely chopped

1 garlic clove, finely chopped

½ tsp dried chile flakes

4 plum tomatoes, peeled and
coarsely chopped

2 eggs

salt and pepper

Heat the oil in a large nonstick frying pan over a campfire, stove, or barbecue. Add the onion and cook until golden. Add the bell peppers, garlic, and chile flakes, and cook until the bell peppers are softened.

Stir in the tomatoes, season to taste with salt and pepper, and simmer over low heat for 10 minutes.

Using the back of a spoon, make 2 depressions in the mixture in the frying pan. Break the eggs into the depressions, cover, and cook for 3–4 minutes, until the eggs are set. Serve.

Scrambled Eggs with Smoked Salmon

Serves 4

8 eggs

⅓ cup light cream

2 tbsp chopped fresh dill,
plus extra for garnishing

3½ oz/100 g smoked salmon,
cut into small pieces

2 tbsp butter

4 slices rustic bread, toasted

salt and pepper

Break the eggs into a large bowl and whisk together with the cream and dill. Season to taste with salt and pepper. Add the smoked salmon and mix to combine.

Melt the butter in a large nonstick frying pan over a campfire, stove, or barbecue and pour in the egg-and-smoked salmon mixture. Using a wooden spatula, gently scrape the egg away from the sides of the frying pan as it starts to set and swirl the frying pan slightly until the uncooked egg fills the surface. When the eggs are almost cooked but still creamy, remove from the heat and spoon onto the prepared toast. Serve at once, garnished with chopped dill.

Chipotle Beans & Hot Dogs

Serves 4

1 tbsp vegetable oil

8 hot dogs

1 lb 13 oz/830 g canned baked beans

½ tsp chipotle paste

scant 1 cup shredded sharp cheddar cheese

salt and pepper

Heat the oil in a nonstick frying pan over a campfire, stove, or barbecue and cook the hot dogs for 15–20 minutes, or until thoroughly cooked. Remove from the pan and cut into thick pieces.

Add the baked beans and chipotle paste to the frying pan, and heat for 4–5 minutes, stirring, until hot. Return the hot dogs to the frying pan to reheat. Season to taste.

Serve the bean and hot dogs with the shredded cheese sprinkled over the top.

Skillet Bread

Makes about 8

2¼ cups self-rising flour
½ tsp salt
¾ cup milk
2 tbsp honey
olive oil, for greasing
butter and jelly, to serve

Put the flour in a bowl, add the salt, and make a well in the center.

Combine the milk and honey, add to the flour, and, using a knife, mix well to form a dough. Using your hands, shape the dough into 8 small patties.

Lightly oil a nonstick frying pan and cook the patties over a campfire, stove, or around the edge of a barbecue for about 10 minutes, until a crust has formed and the center is just cooked (test by tapping the bottom with your fingers. If it sounds hollow, then it is cooked). Turn regularly to prevent burning.

Slice in half and serve with butter and jelly.

Apple Pancakes with Maple Syrup

Makes 18

scant 1½ cups self-rising flour

½ cup superfine sugar

1 tsp ground cinnamon

1 egg

scant 1 cup milk

2 apples, peeled and grated

2 tsp butter

Maple Syrup Butter

1 tbsp butter

3 tbsp maple syrup,
plus extra for drizzling

Mix the flour, sugar, and cinnamon together in a bowl and make a well in the center. Beat the egg and the milk together and pour into the well. Using a wooden spoon, gently incorporate the dry ingredients into the liquid until well combined, then stir in the grated apple.

Heat the butter in a large nonstick frying pan over a campfire, stove, or barbecue, until melting and bubbling. Add tablespoons of the pancake mixture to form 3½-inch/9-cm circles. Cook each pancake for about 1 minute, until it starts to bubble lightly on the top and looks set, then flip it over and cook the other side for 30 seconds, or until cooked through and golden brown. Remove from the frying pan and keep warm. Repeat the process until all of the pancake batter has been used up (it is not necessary to add extra butter).

To make the maple syrup butter, melt the butter with the maple syrup in a pan over low heat and stir until combined. To serve, place the pancakes on serving dishes and spoon over the flavored butter. Serve with more maple syrup drizzled over the pancakes. Enjoy!

French Toast with Maple Syrup

Serves 4–6

6 eggs

¾ cup milk

¼ tsp ground cinnamon

12 slices day-old challah or plain white bread

4 tbsp butter or margarine

½–1 tbsp sunflower-seed or corn oil

salt

maple syrup, to serve

Break the eggs into a large, shallow bowl and beat together with the milk and cinnamon. Season with salt. Add the bread slices and press them down so that they are covered on both sides with the egg mixture. Leave the bread to stand for 1–2 minutes to soak up the egg mixture, turning the slices over once.

Melt the butter with the oil in a large nonstick frying pan over a campfire, stove, or barbecue. Add as many bread slices as will fit in a single layer to the frying pan and cook for 2–3 minutes, until golden brown.

Turn the bread slices over and cook until golden brown on the other side. Wrap the cooked bread in aluminum foil to keep warm and repeat with the remaining bread, adding extra oil if necessary.

Serve the toast with the maple syrup.

Lunchtime

Bread & Tomato Soup

Serves 6

1 lb/450 g two-day-old
crusty bread

2 lb 4 oz/1 kg ripe plum
tomatoes

4 tbsp olive oil

4 garlic cloves, crushed

scant 2½ cups boiling water

1 bunch of fresh basil

salt and pepper

6 tbsp extra virgin olive oil,
to serve

Cut the bread into slices and then cubes (you can remove some of the crusts if you like) and let dry out for 30 minutes. Meanwhile, peel the tomatoes and cut into chunks.

Gently heat the oil in a large pan over a campfire, stove, or barbecue, add the garlic, and cook over medium heat, stirring, for 1 minute without browning. Add the tomatoes and simmer gently for 20–30 minutes, or until the mixture has thickened.

Add the bread and stir until it has absorbed the liquid. Stir in the boiling water until you have a thick soupy mixture. Season well with salt and pepper.

Remove the basil leaves from their stems and tear any large leaves into pieces. Stir the basil into the soup.

Serve warm with a tablespoonful of extra virgin olive oil sprinkled over each bowl.

Chicken Noodle Soup

Serves 4–6

2 skinless chicken breasts

5 cups water or chicken stock

3 carrots, peeled and cut into
¼-inch/5-mm slices

3 oz/85 g spaghetti
(or other small noodles)

salt and pepper

Place the chicken breasts in a large saucepan, add the water,
and bring to a simmer over a campfire, stove, or barbecue. Skim
any foam from the surface, if necessary. Remove the chicken from
the stock and keep warm.

Continue to simmer the stock, add the carrots and spaghetti,
and cook for 4–5 minutes.

Thinly slice or shred the chicken and add to the soup. Season to
taste with salt and pepper and serve in mugs.

Cheesy Corn Fritters

Makes 8–10 small fritters

1 egg

generous ¾ cup milk

¾ cup all-purpose flour

½ tsp baking powder

2¾ oz/75 g canned corn, drained without added salt or sugar, drained

¼ cup shredded cheddar cheese

1 tsp snipped fresh chives

2 tsp sunflower oil, for pan-frying

Put the egg and milk into a small bowl and beat with a fork. Add the flour and baking powder and beat until smooth. Stir in the corn, cheese, and chives. Heat a little sunflower oil in a frying pan over a campfire, stove, or barbecue and drop either teaspoonfuls or tablespoonfuls of the batter into it. Cook for 1–2 minutes on each side, until the fritters are puffed up and golden.

Drain on paper towels and serve.

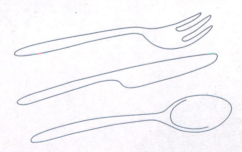

Spinach & Mozzarella O'melet

Serves 4

1 tbsp oil

1 tbsp butter

4 eggs, beaten lightly

1½ oz/40 g mozzarella, thinly sliced and cut into bite-size pieces

small handful baby spinach, stalks removed

salt and pepper

Heat the oil in a large nonstick frying pan over a campfire, stove, or barbecue. Add the butter and, when it sizzles, pour in the eggs. Season with salt and pepper, then stir gently with the back of a fork until large flakes form. Let cook for a few seconds, then tilt the frying pan and lift the edges of the mixture with a spatula, so that the uncooked egg flows underneath.

Scatter the cheese and spinach over the top, and let cook for a few seconds. Once the surface starts to solidify, carefully fold the omelet in half. Cook for a few seconds, pressing the surface with a spatula. Turn the omelet over and cook for another few seconds, until the cheese is soft and the spinach is wilted.

Slip the omelet onto a plate and slice into segments. Serve warm or cold.

Tomato Bruschetta

Serves 4

8 slices of crusty bread, toasted

4 garlic cloves, halved

8 plum tomatoes, peeled and
diced

extra virgin olive oil,
for drizzling

salt and pepper

fresh basil leaves, to garnish

Rub each piece of toast with half a garlic clove.

Divide the diced tomatoes among the toasts. Season to taste with
salt and pepper and drizzle with olive oil. Serve immediately,
garnished with basil leaves.

Chicken Sandwich with Cheese & Relish

Serves 4

8 thin slices whole wheat or
whole grain bread
2 tsp soft butter
1½ cups cooked sliced chicken
3½ oz/100 g sharp cheddar
cheese
½ cup fruity relish

Heat a nonstick frying pan over a campfire, stove, or barbecue. Spread one side of each slice of bread with a little butter.

To make each sandwich, place one slice of bread buttered side down in the hot frying pan and add one-quarter of the chicken and cheese. Spread 2 tablespoons of the relish over the unbuttered side of the other slice of bread, place on top of the sandwich, relish side down, and press down firmly.

Cook over a moderate heat for 2–3 minutes on each side so that the bread is lightly toasted and the cheese melted.

Repeat with the remaining ingredients and serve.

Beef & Blue Cheese Wraps

Serves 4

9 oz/250 g sirloin steak

1 tbsp olive oil

4½ oz/125 g blue cheese, such as Gorgonzola, crumbled

1 tbsp mayonnaise

4 wraps, about 10 inches/25 cm in diameter

salt and pepper

Season the steak with salt and pepper.

Preheat a nonstick frying pan until almost smoking over a campfire, stove, or barbecue. Add the oil, then add the steak and seal, cooking for 30 seconds on each side for very rare (or longer according to personal preference). Remove from the frying pan and set aside to rest for a few minutes. Cut into thin strips with a sharp knife.

Mix together the cheese and mayonnaise.

Preheat a nonstick frying pan until almost smoking, add the wraps, 1 at a time, and cook for 10 seconds on each side. This will add some color and soften the wraps. Remove from the pan.

Divide the steak strips evenly among the wraps, placing them along the center of each wrap. Top with some of the cheese-and-mayonnaise mixture. Fold in the wraps at the ends, roll up, cut in half diagonally, and serve.

Campfire Quesadillas

Serves 1

2 flour tortillas

1–2 tbsp tomato salsa

¼ cup freshly shredded Manchego or other hard cheese

4 slices chopped chorizo

Heat a nonstick frying pan over a campfire, stove, or barbecue until moderately hot.

Spread 1 of the tortillas with the salsa and place in the frying pan. Top with the cheese and chorizo and then top with the other tortilla. Let cook for 1–2 minutes, until starting to turn golden on the bottom.

Flip the quesadilla over using a knife and cook for an additional 1–2 minutes to let the cheese melt and the bottom of the tortilla brown lightly. Serve immediately.

Herb-Stuffed Trout

Serves 4

4 whole trout, about
12 oz/350 g each, cleaned
olive oil for brushing
1 small bunch flat-leaf parsley
1 small bunch chives
1 lemon, thinly sliced
salt and pepper
lemon wedges, to serve

Arugula Sauce

2 bunches arugula, stalks
discarded, coarsely chopped
juice of ½ lemon
3 tbsp vegetable or fish stock
4 tbsp heavy cream
4 tbsp plain yogurt
salt and pepper

To prepare the trout, make two diagonal slashes on each side in the thickest part of the flesh, about 3½ inches/9 cm apart. Brush all over with olive oil. Stuff the slashes and the body cavity with parsley sprigs, chives, and half slices of lemon. Season with salt and pepper. Oil a large square of aluminum foil and place the trout in it.

For the sauce, put the arugula, lemon juice, and stock in a bowl, season to taste with salt and pepper and mash with the back of a fork until well combined. Pour into a pitcher, stir in the cream and yogurt and mix well.

Cook the trout over a campfire, stove, or barbecue for 5–6 minutes a side, or until the thickest part along the spine is opaque when cut into with a knife.

Carefully remove the trout from the foil, using the tip of a knife to ease the skin away. Serve on plates with lemon wedges and the arugula sauce.

Shrimp & Scallop Skewers

Serves 4–6

24 shrimp
12 large scallops, corals attached
4–5 tbsp olive oil
juice of 1 lime
1 tbsp chopped fresh cilantro
salt and pepper
lime wedges to serve

If using wooden skewers, soak 1 per person in cold water for 30 minutes first to prevent burning.

Shell the shrimp but leave the tails attached. Slit down the back and remove the dark intestinal vein. Remove the tough muscle from the side of the scallops. Slice in half lengthwise through the coral. Combine the olive oil and lime juice in a shallow dish. Add a pinch of salt and pepper. Add the scallops and shrimp and let marinate for 15 minutes.

Reserving the marinade, thread the scallops and shrimp alternately onto 8 wooden skewers. Cook over a campfire, stove, or barbecue for 4–6 minutes, turning and brushing with the marinade, until the shrimp are pink and cooked through.

Arrange on plates, and sprinkle with the cilantro and a little more salt and pepper. Serve with lime wedges.

Grilled Chicken Skewers

Serves 4

4 tbsp smooth peanut butter

generous ⅓ cup soy sauce

4 skinless, boneless chicken
breasts, cut into thin strips

If using wooden skewers, soak 1 per person in cold water for 30 minutes first to prevent burning.

Mix together the peanut butter and soy sauce in a bowl until smooth. Stir in the chicken strips, tossing well to coat in the mixture.

Thread the chicken strips onto the presoaked wooden skewers and cook over a campfire, stove, or barbecue until cooked through. Serve immediately.

Tomato & Mozzarella Stacks

Serves 4

4 large slicing tomatoes,
about 7 oz/200 g each

8 oz/225 g buffalo mozzarella

olive oil, for brushing

24 basil leaves

salt and pepper

Using a sharp serrated knife, cut a thin slice from the top and bottom of each tomato and discard. Slice the rest of the tomato horizontally into three. Slice the mozzarella into thin rounds.

Brush the center of a large square of aluminum foil with oil. Place a tomato slice on the foil, brush with oil, and season with salt and pepper. Add a few basil leaves and a slice of cheese. Continue layering using the second and third tomato slices, seasoning each layer, and finishing with a layer of mozzarella. Fold up the edges of the foil to make a bowl shape. Repeat with the three remaining tomatoes and mozzarella.

Cook over a campfire, stove, or barbecue for 8–10 minutes, until the top tomato slice is heated through and the mozzarella melted. Serve immediately.

Ratatouille with Poached Eggs

Serves 4

2 tbsp olive oil

1 large onion, sliced

2 bell peppers, any color, seeded and thinly sliced

2 zucchini, sliced into thin rounds

1 small eggplant, thinly sliced

2 garlic cloves, chopped

14 oz/400 g canned, chopped tomatoes with herbs, plus extra, if needed

8 small eggs

salt and pepper

Gently heat the oil in a large, lidded, nonstick frying pan over a campfire, stove, or barbecue. Add the onion and bell peppers and cook, stirring frequently, for 4–5 minutes, or until beginning to soften.

Add the zucchini, eggplant, and garlic and cook, stirring, for 2 minutes. Add the tomatoes and season to taste with salt and pepper. Stir and bring to a simmer. Place over low heat, cover, and let simmer gently for 45 minutes, adding a little more of the tomatoes or water if the mixture begins to look dry.

Make 8 wells in the ratatouille and break an egg into each. Re-cover and cook for an additional 10 minutes, or until the egg whites are cooked but the yolks still runny. Serve immediately.

Potato Pancake

Serves 4

1½ lb/675 g waxy potatoes, unpeeled and sliced

1 carrot, diced

3 cups small broccoli florets

5 tbsp butter

2 tbsp vegetable oil

1 red onion, cut into quarters

2 garlic cloves, crushed

6 oz/175 g firm tofu, drained and diced (optional)

2 tbsp chopped fresh sage

¾ cup shredded cheddar cheese

Cook the sliced potatoes in a large pan of boiling water over a campfire, stove, or barbecue for 10 minutes. Drain thoroughly.

Meanwhile, cook the carrot and broccoli florets in a separate pan of boiling water for 5 minutes. Drain.

Heat the butter and oil in a large nonstick frying pan. Add the onion and garlic and cook over low heat for 2–3 minutes. Add half of the potato slices to the frying pan, covering the bottom of the frying pan.

Cover the potato slices with the carrot, broccoli, and the tofu. Sprinkle with half of the sage and cover with the remaining potato slices. Sprinkle the shredded cheese over the top.

Cook over high heat for 8–10 minutes. Cover the frying pan with a piece of aluminum foil and cook for 5–6 minutes, until the cheese melts and browns. Serve immediately.

Pepperoni Muffin Pizzas

Serves 4

¼ cup pizza sauce
(or tomato sauce)

4 whole wheat or white English
muffins, halved

2 tbsp olives, pitted and chopped

3 button mushrooms,
finely sliced

3½ oz/100 g pepperoni,
thinly sliced

4½ oz/125 g mozzarella cheese,
thinly sliced

Spread the pizza sauce over the cut sides of the halved muffins.

Sprinkle over the olives, mushrooms, and pepperoni.

Lay the mozzarella over the toppings and place the English muffins (about 4 halves at a time) in a large nonstick frying pan. Tightly cover with foil and place over a campfire, stove, or barbecue for 8–10 minutes, checking regularly to ensure that the bottoms are not burning and the cheese is melting. Serve immediately.

Hearty Dinners

Chicken with Tarragon Butter

Serves 4

4 skinless, boneless chicken
breasts, about 8 oz/225 g each

olive oil, for brushing

Tarragon Butter	Marinade
½ cup (1 stick) unsalted butter	1½ tbsp lemon juice
⅓ cup chopped fresh tarragon	2 tbsp water
1 shallot, finely chopped	1 tsp sugar
	1 tsp salt
	3 tbsp olive oil

To make the tarragon butter, mash the butter until soft, then add the remaining ingredients, mixing well. Set aside.

Slice the chicken breasts lengthwise to make 8 portions. Whisk together the marinade ingredients and pour into a resealable bag with the chicken, let stand for 30 minutes, shaking the bag halfway through.

Drain the chicken and discard the marinade. Pat dry and lightly brush with oil. Place the chicken on a rack and cover with aluminum foil. Cook over a campfire, stove, or barbecue for 5–6 minutes, until cooked, turn, and cook the other side for 4–5 minutes, or until no longer pink when cut into.

Place in a warmed dish, cover with foil, and let rest for 5 minutes. Serve with the tarragon butter melted over the top.

Lamb Stew

Serves 4–6

3 lb/1.3 kg potatoes, peeled
2 lb/1 kg lean lamb, cubed
1 lb/500 g onions, thinly sliced
4 cups water
salt and pepper

Thinly slice half the potatoes. Make alternating layers of lamb, onions, and sliced potatoes in a large pan with a lid, seasoning each layer with salt and pepper. Pour in the water so that the layers are just covered.

Bring to a boil over a campfire, stove, or barbecue. Place over low heat, cover, and simmer for 1³/4 hours. Cut the remaining potatoes into quarters and place on top of the stew to steam. Re-cover the pan and simmer for an additional 45 minutes, or until the potato quarters are tender.

Arrange the steamed potatoes around the outside of a warmed serving dish. Place the meat, onions, and sliced potatoes in the center. Taste the cooking liquid and adjust the seasoning, if necessary, then spoon it over the meat and serve immediately.

Chicken & Apricot Casserole

Serves 4

¼ cup all-purpose flour

4 chicken portions

4 tbsp olive oil

2 cups dried apricots, soaked overnight in 2½ cups water

salt and pepper

Spread out the flour on a plate and season with salt and pepper. Roll the chicken portions in the flour to coat, shaking off any excess. Set aside the remaining seasoned flour.

Gently heat the oil in a pan over a campfire, stove, or barbecue. Add the chicken and cook, turning occasionally for 8–10 minutes, until golden brown. Remove with a slotted spoon and set aside.

Drain the apricots, setting aside the soaking liquid. Add the reserved flour to the casserole dish and cook over low heat, stirring continuously, for 2 minutes. Gradually stir in the reserved soaking liquid and bring to a boil, while stirring continuously.

Add the apricots and return the chicken to the casserole dish. Cover and simmer gently for 45 minutes, or until the chicken is tender and cooked through. Test by piercing the thickest part with the point of a knife. If the juices run clear, the chicken is ready. Serve immediately.

Creamy Ricotta, Mint & Garlic Pasta

Serves 4

10½ oz/300 g short fresh pasta
e.g. ziti or penne

heaping ½ cup ricotta cheese

1–2 roasted garlic cloves from a
jar, finely chopped

⅔ cup heavy cream

1 tbsp chopped fresh mint

salt and pepper

Cook the pasta in a large pan of boiling salted water over a campfire, stove, or barbecue, until tender but still firm to the bite.

Beat the ricotta, garlic, cream, and chopped mint together in a bowl until smooth.

Drain the cooked pasta then turn back into the pan. Pour in the cheese mixture and toss together.

Season with pepper and serve immediately.

Bad Weather Blues
(And How To Beat Them)

People can be pretty resourceful when it comes to dealing with the weather and its unpredictability. However, when you're camping and the weather is bad, sometimes a little bit of planning ahead can make all the difference. Here are a few ideas on how to overcome those bad weather blues.

Before you leave, do some research on the Internet about places of interest nearby. Print off some info and bring it with you on your camping trip.

Head to the nearest library. Here you can find out loads of local info, talk to the staff, and use the Internet if you need to.

Pack a thermos of hot chocolate and a kite on a blustery day.

Write a vacation diary. Popular with all ages, a simple journal with a few paragraphs about your activities each day and some postcards stuck in will be great to look back on in years to come.

Play a few games in the tent if the weather is really bad. Charades and board games are always a hit. Or try making shadow puppets with a flashlight on the inside of the tent at night.

Penne Pasta with Sausage

Serves 4–6

2 tbsp olive oil

1 red onion, coarsely chopped

2 garlic cloves, coarsely chopped

6 Italian sausages, skinned and
the meat crumbled

½ tsp dried chile flakes

2 tbsp chopped fresh oregano

14 oz/400 g canned chopped
tomatoes

12 oz/350 g dried penne

salt and pepper

Gently heat the oil in a large pan over a campfire, stove, or barbecue. Add the onion and cook, stirring frequently, for 6–8 minutes, or until starting to brown. Add the garlic and the crumbled sausages and cook for 8–10 minutes, breaking up the sausages with a wooden spoon.

Add the chile flakes and oregano and stir well. Pour in the tomatoes and bring to a boil. Move the pan to a lower area of heat and simmer for 4–5 minutes, or until reduced and thickened. Season to taste with salt and pepper.

Meanwhile, bring a large pan of salted water to a boil. Add the penne and stir well, then return to a boil and cook for 10–12 minutes, or according to the package directions, until al dente or just tender but still firm to the bite. Drain well and return to the pan.

Pour the sauce into the pasta and stir well. Serve.

Spicy Potatoes & Spinach

Serves 4

4 tomatoes

2 tbsp vegetable oil

2 onions, cut into thick wedges

1 garlic clove, chopped

2 tbsp ground coriander

1 lb/450 g potatoes,
cut into chunks

2½ cups vegetable stock

1 tbsp Thai red Curry Paste

8 oz/225 g spinach leaves

salt and pepper

Put the tomatoes in a heatproof bowl and cover with boiling water. Leave for 2–3 minutes, then plunge into cold water and peel off the skins. Cut each tomato into quarters and remove and discard the seeds and central core. Set aside.

Gently heat the oil in a large nonstick frying pan over a campfire, stove, or barbecue. Add the onions and garlic and fry for 2–3 minutes, until starting to soften. Add the coriander and potatoes and fry for 2–3 minutes. Add the stock and curry paste, season, and bring to a boil, stirring occasionally. Move the frying pan to a lower area of heat and gently simmer for 10–15 minutes until the potatoes are tender.

Add the spinach and the tomato quarters and cook, stirring, for 1 minute, or until the spinach has wilted. Serve immediately.

Mushroom Stroganoff

Serves 4

2 tbsp butter

1 onion, finely chopped

1 lb/450 g button mushrooms, quartered

1 tsp tomato paste

1 tsp stone ground mustard

⅔ cup sour cream

salt and pepper

Heat the butter in a large frying pan over a campfire, stove, or barbecue. Add the onion and cook gently for 5–10 minutes, until softened.

Add the mushrooms to the frying pan and fry for a few minutes, until they start to soften. Stir in the tomato paste and mustard, then add the sour cream. Cook gently, stirring constantly, for 5 minutes.

Season to taste with salt and pepper, transfer to bowls, and serve.

Hamburgers with chili & Basil

Serves 4

1 lb 7 oz/650 g ground beef

1 red bell pepper, seeded and
finely chopped

1 garlic clove, finely chopped

2 small red chiles, seeded and
finely chopped

1 tbsp chopped fresh basil, plus
extra leaves to garnish

salt and pepper

hamburger buns, to serve

Put the ground beef, red bell pepper, garlic, chiles, and chopped basil into a bowl and mix until well combined. Season to taste with salt and pepper. Using your hands, form the mixture into 4 patties.

Cook over a campfire, stove, or barbecue for 5–8 minutes on each side, or until cooked through. Garnish with a few basil leaves and serve in hamburger buns.

Veggie Burgers

Serves 4

15 oz/420 g canned red kidney beans, drained

14½ oz/410 g canned cooked chickpeas, drained

1 egg yolk

1 cup fresh breadcrumbs

3 scallions, finely chopped

salt and pepper

hamburger buns, sour cream, lettuce, and sliced tomatoes, to serve

Place the beans and chickpeas in a bowl, stir in the egg yolk, breadcrumbs, and scallions, and season. Mash together using the back of a fork. The mixture should be mashed just enough so that everything sticks together but retains some of its texture.

Using your hands, form the mixture into 4 patties.

Cook over a campfire, stove, or barbecue for 5–8 minutes on each side, or until cooked through.

Serve in hamburger buns with a spoonful of sour cream, plenty of fresh crisp lettuce, and some sliced tomatoes.

Honey-Glazed Pork Chops

Serves 4

4 lean pork chops
corn oil, for oiling
salt and pepper

Honey Glaze
4 tbsp honey
5 tbsp orange juice
2 tbsp olive oil

Season the pork chops with salt and pepper to taste. Set aside.

To make the glaze, place the honey, orange juice, and half the olive oil in a small pan. Heat gently over a campfire, stove, or barbecue, stirring continuously, until blended.

Heat the remaining olive oil and corn oil in a large frying pan and cook the pork chops for 5 minutes on each side.

Brush the chops with the glaze and cook for an additional 2–4 minutes on each side, basting frequently with the glaze.

Transfer the pork chops to serving plates and serve hot.

Spicy Tomato Chicken Skewers

Serves 4

1 lb 2 oz/500 g skinless,
boneless chicken breasts

3 tbsp tomato paste

2 tbsp honey

2 tbsp Worcestershire sauce

1 tbsp chopped fresh rosemary

16 cherry tomatoes

Using a sharp knife, cut the chicken into 1-inch/
2.5-cm chunks and place in a bowl. Mix the tomato
paste, honey, Worcestershire sauce, and rosemary
together in a separate bowl, then add to the chicken,
stirring to coat evenly.

If using wooden skewers, soak 2 per person in cold
water for 30 minutes first to prevent burning. Thread
the chicken pieces and cherry tomatoes alternately
onto the skewers.

Spoon over any remaining glaze and cook the
skewers over a campfire, stove, or barbecue,
turning occasionally, until the chicken is cooked
through. Serve immediately.

Yakitori Vegetable Skewers

Serves 4

1 large zucchini, sliced

4 scallions, sliced diagonally

1 orange bell pepper,
seeded and cubed

3½ oz/100 g button mushrooms,
wiped clean

8 cherry tomatoes

Yakitori Sauce

1 tbsp soy sauce

1 tbsp honey

1 tbsp rice vinegar

If using wooden skewers, soak 1 per person in cold water for 30 minutes first to prevent burning.

Divide all the vegetables between the wooden skewers, alternating the pieces to make 4 skewers.

Mix together the yakitori sauce ingredients and drizzle over the skewers. Cook the skewers over a campfire, stove, or barbecue for about 10–12 minutes until the vegetables are just tender, but not soft.

Baked Salmon with Artichoke

Serves 4

4 salmon steaks,
about 6 oz/175 g each

½ lemon, sliced

1 onion, sliced into rings

4 fresh dill sprigs

4 canned artichoke hearts,
drained

4 tbsp olive oil

4 tbsp chopped fresh
flat-leaf parsley

salt and pepper

Cut out 4 squares of aluminum foil, each large enough to enclose a fish steak. Place the salmon on the foil and top with the lemon slices, onion rings, and dill sprigs. Place an artichoke heart on each salmon steak.

Fold up the sides of the foil. Sprinkle 1 tablespoon of olive oil and 1 tablespoon of parsley into each package and season with a little salt and pepper. Fold over the edges of the foil securely.

Cook the wrapped fish over a campfire, stove, or barbecue for 15 minutes, turning once. Transfer the packages to plates and unwrap. Serve immediately.

Sun-Dried Tomato Risotto

Serves 6

about 12 sun-dried tomatoes

2 tbsp olive oil

1 large onion, finely chopped

4–6 garlic cloves, finely chopped

2 cups risotto rice

6¼ cups simmering chicken or vegetable stock

2 tbsp chopped fresh flat-leaf parsley

1 cup freshly grated Parmesan cheese

salt and pepper

Place the sun-dried tomatoes in a heatproof bowl and pour over enough boiling water to cover. Set aside to soak for 30 minutes, or until soft and supple. Drain and pat dry with paper towels, then shred thinly and set aside.

Gently heat the oil in a large pan over a campfire, stove, or barbecue. Add the onion and cook, stirring occasionally, for 2 minutes or until starting to soften. Add the garlic and cook for an additional 15 seconds. Place over a low heat, add the rice, and mix to coat in oil. Cook, stirring constantly for 2–3 minutes, or until the grains are translucent.

Gradually add the hot stock, a spoonful at a time. Stir constantly and add more liquid as the rice absorbs each addition. Place over a low heat so that the liquid bubbles. After about 15 minutes, stir in the sun-dried tomatoes, stirring constantly, until the risotto has been cooking for 20 minutes or until all the liquid is absorbed and the rice is creamy.

Remove the pan from the heat and stir in the chopped parsley and half the Parmesan cheese. Spoon into bowls and sprinkle the remaining Parmesan on top. Serve immediately.

Chicken Risotto with Saffron

Serves 4

½ cup (1 stick) butter

2 lb/900 g skinless, boneless chicken breasts, thinly sliced

1 large onion, chopped

2⅔ cups risotto rice

⅔ cup white wine

1 tsp crumbled saffron threads

generous 5½ cups boiling chicken stock

½ cup freshly grated Parmesan cheese

salt and pepper

Melt 4 tablespoons of the butter in a deep pan over a campfire, stove, or barbecue. Add the chicken and onion and cook, stirring frequently, for 8 minutes, or until golden brown.

Add the rice and mix to coat in the butter. Cook, stirring constantly for 2–3 minutes, or until the grains are translucent. Add the wine and cook, stirring constantly, for 1 minute, until reduced. Mix the saffron with ¼ cup of the hot stock. Add the liquid to the rice and cook, stirring constantly, until it is absorbed.

Gradually add the remaining hot stock, a spoonful at a time. Stir constantly and add more liquid as the rice absorbs each addition. Cook for 20 minutes, or until all the liquid is absorbed and the rice is creamy. Season to taste.

Remove the risotto from the heat and add the remaining butter. Mix well, then stir in the Parmesan until it melts. Spoon the risotto into bowls and serve immediately.

Easy Calzone

Serves 4

4 flour or corn tortillas

½ cup pizza sauce
(or tomato sauce)

1½ cups cooked chicken,
finely shredded

7 oz/200 g mozzarella cheese,
cut into small pieces

handful basil leaves, torn

salt and pepper

Evenly spread one side of each tortilla with 2 tablespoons of pizza sauce. Top each tortilla with one-quarter of the chicken, mozzarella, and basil leaves and season.

Heat a nonstick frying pan over a campfire, stove, or barbecue.

Cook one calzone at a time in the frying pan by first cooking the tortilla for 2 minutes. Then fold in half, press down the edges well to seal, and cook for an additional 1 minute on each side. The center should be piping hot and the mozzarella starting to melt.

Repeat with the remaining 3 tortillas and serve.

Something On The Side

Garlic Bread

Serves 6

¾ cup (1½ sticks) butter, softened

3 cloves garlic, crushed

2 tbsp chopped fresh parsley

pepper

1 large or 2 small loaves
of French bread

Mix together the butter, garlic, and parsley in a bowl until well combined. Season with pepper to taste and mix well.

Make several lengthwise cuts in the bread, being careful not to cut all the way through.

Spread the flavored butter over one side of each cut and place the loaf on a large sheet of aluminum foil.

Wrap the bread well in the foil and cook over a campfire, stove, or barbecue for 10–15 minutes, until the butter melts and the bread is piping hot. Serve as an accompaniment to a wide range of dishes.

Stuffed Baked Potatoes

Serves 4

4 large potatoes, scrubbed

1 tbsp olive oil

salt

Tuna and Sour Cream Stuffing

14 oz/400 g canned tuna

8 tbsp sour cream

pepper

Herbed Sausage and Onion Stuffing

1 tbsp olive oil

I red onion, finely chopped

8 pork sausages

handful flat-leaf parsley, finely chopped

pepper

tomato relish or salsa, to serve

Use some clean paper towels to rub the potatoes with a little olive oil and sprinkle with salt to coat lightly.

Tightly wrap the potatoes in aluminum foil and cook over a campfire or barbecue (toward the edge, away from the hottest part), for about one hour. The cooking time will depend on the size of potato and the strength of the heat from the fire or barbecue. The potato is ready when it yields to the tip of a sharp knife.

To make the tuna-and-sour cream stuffing, simply drain the tuna and serve on the cooked opened potato. Drizzle over the the sour cream and top with pepper.

To make the herbed sausage-and-onion stuffing, heat the oil in a nonstick frying pan over a campfire, stove, or barbecue and sauté the onion for 5–10 minutes. Squeeze the sausage meat out of its casing and add to the pan. Continue to cook until it is browned and thoroughly cooked, breaking it up with a fork as you cook it. Stir in the parsley. Serve the sausage meat over the baked potato with salsa. Season to taste and enjoy.

Meatballs on Sticks

Serves 8

4 pork and herb sausages

4 oz/115 g fresh ground beef

1½ cups fresh white breadcrumbs

1 onion, finely chopped

2 tbsp chopped mixed fresh herbs, such as parsley, thyme, and sage

1 egg

corn oil, for brushing

salt and pepper

Soak the toothpicks in cold water for 30 minutes first to prevent burning.

Remove the sausage meat from the casings, place in a large bowl and break up with a fork. Add the ground beef, breadcrumbs, onion, herbs, and egg. Season to taste with salt and pepper and stir well with a wooden spoon until thoroughly mixed.

Form the mixture into small balls, about the size of a golf ball, between the palms of your hands. Spear each one with a toothpick and brush with oil.

Cook over a campfire, barbecue, or stove, turning frequently and brushing with more oil as necessary, for 10 minutes, or until cooked through. Transfer to a large serving plate and serve immediately.

Sweet Potato Fries

Serves 4

¾ cup olive oil

2 medium sweet potatoes, peeled and cut into thin sticks

2 tsp Cajun spice

salt

mayonnaise, to serve

Heat the oil in a nonstick frying pan over a campfire, stove, or barbecue.

Add the sweet potato sticks, scatter over the seasoning, and toss well. Gently fry for about 10–12 minutes, turning regularly until just tender. Serve scattered with salt and some mayonnaise.

Campfire Nachos

Serves 4

4 oz/100 g salted tortilla chips
1 cup shredded cooked chicken
¾ cup shredded cheddar cheese
pepper
⅓ cup tomato salsa and
⅓ cup sour cream, to serve

Place a large piece of aluminum foil in the bottom of a nonstick frying pan and place over a campfire, stove, or barbecue.

Place the tortilla chips in a single layer on the foil. Scatter over the chicken and cheese. Cover the frying pan with a lid or aluminum foil.

Cook the nachos for about 10–15 minutes, until the cheese is just melting.

Season with pepper and serve with tomato salsa and sour cream.

Campfire Roasted Balsamic & Honey Onions

Serves 4

4 red onions, peeled and cut into chunky wedges

4 tsp honey

4 tbsp balsamic vinegar

1 tsp fresh thyme, finely chopped

salt and pepper

Divide the onion wedges between four squares of heavy duty aluminum foil. Bring up the sides of the foil a little.

Drizzle the honey and balsamic vinegar over the onions, add the thyme, and season.

Loosely seal the packages and cook over a campfire or barbecue for 15–20 minutes, until the onions are tender.

Made-from-scratch Baked Beans

Serves 4–6

1 lb 5 oz/600 g fresh
borlotti beans
4 large leaves fresh sage, torn
1 tbsp olive oil
1 large onion, thinly sliced
1¼ cups good-quality
tomato sauce
salt and pepper

Shell the borlotti beans. Bring a saucepan of water to a boil over a campfire, stove, or barbecue and add the beans and torn sage leaves. Bring back to a boil, and simmer for about 12 minutes, or until tender. Drain and set aside.

Gently heat the oil in a large frying pan. Add the onion and cook, stirring occasionally, for about 5 minutes, until softened and translucent but not browned. Stir the tomato sauce into the frying pan with the cooked borlotti beans and the fresh sage leaves.

Bring to a boil, stirring. Place over a low heat, partially cover, and simmer for about 10 minutes, or until the sauce has slightly reduced.

Adjust the seasoning, transfer to a serving bowl, and serve hot.

Peas with Pearl Onions

Serves 4

1 tbsp unsalted butter

1 cup pearl onions

2 lb/900 g fresh or canned peas, shelled

½ cup water

2 tbsp all-purpose flour

⅔ cup heavy cream

1 tbsp chopped fresh parsley

1 tbsp lemon juice

salt and pepper

Melt the butter in a large, heavy pan over a campfire, stove, or barbecue. Add the whole pearl onions and cook, stirring occasionally, for 5 minutes. Add the peas and cook, stirring constantly, for an additional 3 minutes, then add the measured water and bring to a boil. Place over a low heat, partially cover, and simmer for 10 minutes.

Beat the flour into the cream. Remove the pan from the heat, stir in the cream mixture and parsley, and season to taste with salt and pepper.

Return the pan to the heat and cook, stirring gently but constantly, for about 3 minutes, until thickened.

Stir the lemon juice into the sauce and serve the peas immediately.

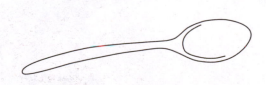

Mixed Potato Pancakes

Serves 4

11½ oz/325 g potatoes
11½ oz/325 g sweet potatoes
4 tbsp sunflower oil
3 tbsp butter
salt

Parboil the ordinary potatoes in a large pan of salted water for 10 minutes, then drain and let cool. Meanwhile, peel and coarsely grate the sweet potatoes into a bowl. When the parboiled potatoes have cooled, peel and coarsely grate into another bowl.

Divide the potatoes and the sweet potatoes separately into 4 equal portions and shape each portion into a pattie about ½ inch/1 cm thick, pressing them together firmly.

Heat half the oil with half the butter in a heavy-bottom frying pan. Add the potato rösti and cook over medium heat for 5 minutes, or until crisp and golden on the undersides. Turn them carefully with a spatula, pat into shape if necessary, and cook for an additional 5 minutes, or until golden brown on the second side. Remove from the frying pan and keep warm.

Heat the remaining oil and butter in the frying pan. Add the sweet potato rösti and cook for 5 minutes on each side as before. Remove from the pan and serve both types of potato rösti immediately.

Potato Salad with Herbs

Serves 4–6

1 lb 2 oz/500 g new potatoes

16 vine-ripened cherry tomatoes, halved

½ cup pitted and coarsely chopped black olives

4 scallions, finely sliced

2 tbsp chopped fresh mint

2 tbsp chopped fresh parsley

2 tbsp chopped fresh cilantro

juice of 1 lemon

3 tbsp extra virgin olive oil

salt and pepper

Cook the potatoes in a pan of lightly salted boiling water over a campfire, stove, or barbecue, for 15 minutes, or until tender. Drain, then let cool slightly before peeling off the skins. Cut into halves or quarters, depending on the size of the potato. Then combine with the tomatoes, olives, scallions, and herbs in a salad bowl.

Mix the lemon juice and oil together in a small bowl or pitcher and pour over the potato salad. Season to taste with salt and pepper before serving.

Crispy Bacon & Spinach Salad

Serves 4

4 tbsp olive oil

4 slices bacon, chopped

1 slice white bread, crusts removed, cut into cubes

1 lb/450 g fresh spinach, torn or shredded

Heat 2 tablespoons of the olive oil in a large frying pan over a campfire, stove, or barbecue. Add the chopped bacon to the frying pan and cook for 3–4 minutes, or until crisp. Remove with a slotted spoon, draining carefully, and set aside.

Toss the cubes of bread in the fat remaining in the frying pan over high heat for about 4 minutes, or until crisp and golden. Remove the croutons with a slotted spoon, draining carefully, and set them aside.

Add the remaining oil to the frying pan and heat. Toss the spinach in the oil over high heat for about 3 minutes, or until it has just wilted. Turn into a serving bowl and sprinkle with the bacon and croutons. Serve immediately.

Corn on the Cob with Blue Cheese Dressing

Serves 6

5 oz/140 g blue cheese
⅔ cup cream cheese
½ cup Greek yogurt
6 ears of corn on the cob
salt and pepper

Crumble the blue cheese, then place in a bowl. Beat with a wooden spoon until creamy. Beat in the cream cheese until thoroughly blended. Gradually beat in the yogurt and season to taste with salt and pepper. Cover with plastic wrap and set aside.

Fold back the husks on each corn and remove the silks. Smooth the husks back into place. Cut out 6 rectangles of aluminum foil, each large enough to enclose an ear of corn. Wrap the corn in the foil.

Cook the corn over hot coals, turning frequently, for 15–20 minutes. Unwrap the corn and discard the foil. Peel back the husk on one side of each and trim off with a sharp knife or kitchen scissors. Serve immediately with the blue cheese dressing.

Garlic Mashed Potatoes

Serves 4

2 lb/900 g starchy potatoes, peeled and cut into chunks

8 garlic cloves, crushed

⅔ cup milk

6 tbsp butter

salt and pepper

Put the potatoes into a large pan. Add enough water to cover and a pinch of salt. Bring to a boil over a campfire, stove, or barbecue and cook for 10 minutes. Add the garlic and cook for an additional 10–15 minutes, or until the potatoes are tender.

Drain the potatoes and garlic, reserving 3 tablespoons of the cooking liquid. Return the reserved cooking liquid to the saucepan, then add the milk and bring to simmering point. Add the butter, return the potatoes and garlic to the pan, and remove from the heat. Mash thoroughly with a potato masher.

Season the potato mixture to taste and beat thoroughly with a wooden spoon until light and fluffy. Serve immediately.

Baked Brie

Serves 4

1 whole Brie (about 7 oz/200 g)
2 cloves garlic, thinly sliced
2 sprigs rosemary,
cut into small pieces
¼ cup white wine (optional)
salt and pepper
crusty French bread, to serve

Remove the Brie from its wrapper and place on a piece of heavy duty aluminum foil.

Make about 8–10 small incisions in the surface of the cheese using the tip of a small sharp knife.

Push the garlic slices and rosemary sprigs into the incisions and then drizzle over the wine (if using). Add a little seasoning.

Loosely seal the foil and then cook directly on the edge of a campfire, stove, or barbecue for about 10–15 minutes, depending on the heat levels, until the cheese has become soft and molten in the centre.

Serve with crusty French bread. A real treat for fans of all things cheesy and gooey.

All Things Sweet

Real Hot Chocolate

Serves 1–2

1½ oz/40 g semisweet chocolate,
broken into pieces
1¼ cups milk

Place the chocolate in a large, heatproof pitcher. Place the milk
in a saucepan and bring to a boil over a campfire, stove,
or barbecue. Pour about 1/3 cup of the milk onto the chocolate
and leave until the chocolate has softened.

Whisk the milk-and-chocolate mixture until smooth. Return the
remaining milk to the heat and return to a boil, then pour onto the
chocolate, whisking constantly.

Pour into warmed mugs or cups and serve immediately.

Quick Tiramisu

Serves 4

1 cup mascarpone cheese or
whole soft cheese

1 egg, separated

2 tbsp plain yogurt

2 tbsp superfine sugar

2 tbsp dark rum

2 tbsp strong black coffee

8 ladyfingers

Place the mascarpone cheese in a large bowl, add the egg yolk and yogurt, and beat until smooth.

Whisk the egg white in a separate dry, grease-free bowl until stiff but not dry, then whisk in the sugar. Carefully fold into the cheese mixture. Divide half the mixture between 4 glasses.

Mix the rum and coffee together in a shallow dish. Dip the ladyfingers into the rum mixture, break them in half, or into smaller pieces if necessary, and divide among the glasses.

Stir any remaining coffee mixture into the remaining cheese mixture and divide between the glasses. Serve immediately.

Fruit Skewers

Serves 4

a selection of fruit, such
as apricots, peaches, figs,
strawberries, mangoes,
pineapple, bananas, dates,
and papaya, prepared and/
or cut into chunks

maple syrup

1¾ oz/50 g semisweet chocolate,
broken into chunks

If using wooden skewers, soak 1 per person in cold water for 30 minutes first to prevent burning.

Thread alternate pieces of fruit onto the presoaked wooden skewers. Brush the fruit with a little maple syrup.

Put the chocolate in a heatproof bowl, set the bowl over a pan of barely simmering water, and heat over a campfire, stove, or barbecue, until the chocolate has melted.

Meanwhile, cook the skewers over the campfire, stove, or barbecue for 3 minutes, or until caramelized. Serve drizzled with the melted chocolate.

Orange & Caramel Bananas

Serves 4

½ cup granulated or
superfine sugar

1 tsp vanilla extract

finely grated zest and juice of
1 orange

4 bananas, peeled and
thickly sliced

2 tbsp butter

Put the sugar, vanilla extract, and orange juice in a nonstick frying pan and gently heat over a campfire, stove, or barbecue, until a caramel consistency is formed.

Add the banana slices and cook, shaking the frying pan, for 1–2 minutes, until they are coated with the caramel.

Add the butter to the frying pan and cook for an additional 3 minutes, shaking the frying pan to coat the bananas.

Turn the bananas onto a serving plate and sprinkle with the orange zest. Serve.

Chocolate Rum Bananas

Serves 4

1 tbsp butter
8 oz/225 g semisweet or milk chocolate
4 large bananas
2 tbsp rum
mascarpone cheese, to serve

Take four large squares of aluminum foil and brush them with butter.

Cut the chocolate into very small pieces. Make a careful slit lengthwise in the peel of each banana, and open just wide enough to insert the chocolate. Place the chocolate pieces inside the bananas, along their lengths, then close them up.

Wrap each stuffed banana in a square of foil and cook over a campfire, stove, or barbecue over hot coals for about 5–10 minutes, or until the chocolate has melted inside the bananas. Remove from the heat, place the bananas on individual serving plates, and pour some rum into each banana.

Serve with mascarpone cheese for a truly indulgent treat.

Chocolate Fondue

Serves 6

18 marshmallows

Fondue
9 oz/250 g semisweet chocolate,
broken into pieces
⅔ cup heavy cream

To make the fondue, place the chocolate and cream in a pan and gently heat over a campfire, stove, or barbecue, stirring constantly until the chocolate has melted.

Thread the marshmallows onto wooden or metal skewers and dip into the chocolate fondue.

Crunchy Ginger Apples

Serves 4

2 tbsp lemon juice

2 tbsp butter, melted

2 tbsp raw brown sugar

4 crisp, tart apples, halved, seeded, and cored

¼ cup diced preserved ginger

Place the lemon juice, butter, and raw brown sugar in 3 separate small dishes. Dip the cut side of the apples first in the lemon juice, then in the melted butter, and, finally, in the sugar.

Cook the apples, cut side down, over a campfire, stove, or barbecue for 5 minutes, or until the sugar caramelizes and the apple surfaces are dark. Turn and cook for an additional 5 minutes to blacken the skin. The cooked apples should still retain their crunch.

Arrange the apple halves in individual dishes (allowing 2 halves per serving), cut side up, and spoon diced preserved ginger over each half.

Rice Pudding

Serves 4–6

1 large orange
1 lemon
4¼ cups milk
1¼ cups short-grain rice
½ cup superfine sugar
1 vanilla bean, split
pinch of salt
½ cup heavy cream
light brown sugar,
to serve (optional)

Coarsely grate the rinds from the orange and lemon and set aside. Rinse a saucepan with cold water but do not dry it.

Put the milk and rice in the pan and bring to a boil over a campfire, stove, or barbecue. Place over a low heat and stir in the superfine sugar, vanilla bean, orange and lemon rinds, and salt, and simmer, stirring constantly, until the pudding is thick and creamy and the rice grains are tender—this can take up to 30 minutes, depending on how wide the pan is.

Remove the vanilla bean and stir in the cream. Serve at once, sprinkled with sugar, if using, or cool completely. The pudding will thicken as it cools, so stir in a little extra milk, if necessary, before serving.

Chocolate & Marshmallow S'Mores

Serves 4

8 marshmallows

8 plain cookies or graham crackers

8 small squares milk chocolate

If using wooden skewers, soak 1 per person in cold water for 30 minutes first to prevent burning.

Thread the marshmallows, 2 at a time, onto the presoaked wooden skewers or metal skewers and toast over a campfire or barbecue until they soften.

Place the soft marshmallows onto one cookie, top with the chocolate squares, and sandwich together with another cookie. Repeat with the remaining cookies and marshmallows.

Marshmallow & Peanut Butter S'Mores

Serves 4

4 marshmallows
1 cup peanut butter
8 graham crackers

If using wooden skewers, soak 1 per person in cold water for 30 minutes first to prevent burning.

Thread the marshmallows onto the wooden skewers and toast over a campfire stove, or barbecue until they soften.

Spread 4 of the graham crackers with peanut butter, top each with a marshmallow, and sandwich together with the remaining crackers. Return to the campfire or barbecue until the peanut butter becomes runny. Serve.

Chocolate Marshmallow Fudge

Makes about 50 pieces

4 oz/115 g bittersweet chocolate, broken into pieces

3⅔ cups white mini marshmallows

5 tbsp butter

2 tsp water

¾ cup chopped coarsely blanched almonds

Put the chocolate in a heatproof bowl, place over a pan of simmering water, and heat over a campfire, stove, or barbecue, until the chocolate has melted. Put the marshmallows, butter, and water in a large saucepan and gently heat, stirring frequently, until melted.

Remove the pan from the heat and pour the chocolate into the mixture. Add the almonds and stir until well mixed.

Pour the mixture into a disposable foil container and let cool for 1–2 hours until set.

Raisin No-Bake Cake

Makes about 20 pieces

7 tbsp butter

¼ cup unsweetened cocoa

2⅔ cups crushed graham crackers

⅔ cup raisins or dried cranberries

1 egg, beaten

4 oz/125 g milk chocolate, broken into squares

Melt the butter in a medium pan over a campfire, stove, or barbecue and stir in the cocoa powder.

Remove from the heat and add the crackers and raisins. Stir well and let cool for 5 minutes.

Add the egg and mix again until thoroughly mixed.

Turn the mixture into a disposable foil tin container. Press down well using the back of a spoon.

Put the chocolate in a heatproof bowl, set the bowl over a pan of simmering water, and heat until the chocolate has melted. Spread evenly over the top of the cake and let cool for 1–2 hours, until set. Cut into squares and keep in an airtight container.

Brazil Nut Brittle

Makes about 20 pieces

sunflower oil, for brushing

12 oz/350 g semisweet chocolate, broken into pieces

scant ¾ cup chopped Brazil nuts

6 oz/175 g white chocolate, coarsely chopped

6 oz/175 g fudge, coarsely chopped

Brush the bottom and sides of a disposable foil container with oil.

Melt the semisweet chocolate pieces in a medium pan over a campfire, stove, or barbecue. Add the Brazil nuts, white chocolate, and fudge. Stir briefly to mix then spread into the prepared container.

Let the brittle set, then break up into jagged pieces using the tip of a strong knife.

Popcorn

Serves 4

1–2 tbsp vegetable oil

¼ cup uncooked popcorn kernels

1 tbsp butter

3 tbsp maple syrup

1 tbsp sesame seeds

Heat the oil in a nonstick pan over a campfire, stove, or barbecue.

Carefully add the popcorn kernels to the pan in an even layer and cover with a lid.

Cook the popcorn over a gentle heat, shaking the pan constantly, until the popcorn kernels stop popping.

Pour the popcorn into a large mixing bowl, discarding any kernels that have not popped.

Melt the butter in a small saucepan, then pour in the maple syrup. Bring to a boil, then remove from the heat and cool. Pour the maple syrup sauce over the popcorn, add the sesame seeds and serve.

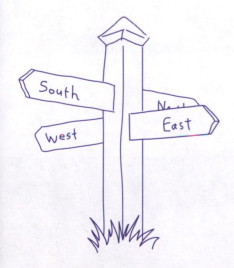

And finally...

A night under the stars will leave you feeling energized, refreshed, and at one with the wonders of nature. In order for others to enjoy the unsurpassable pleasures of camping and to make planning for your next trip that little bit easier, try following these simple suggestions.

Leave your environment exactly as you found it. Collect any garbage and take it home with you (or dispose of it at your campsite if it has facilities).

Collect any dog mess—don't make it someone else's problem.

If you camped with a campfire, make sure it is completely extinguished before you leave—and on a practical note, make sure you don't light it too near your tent.

Remember to separate any garbage that can be recycled. Wash it as well as you can and recycle it at the campsite or take it with you to be recycled at home.

If possible, wait for your tent to dry completely before taking it down—if you can't avoid packing up in the rain, make sure the tent is left out to dry as soon as possible when you return home.

Wipe down the base of the tent with a damp cloth when you get back home, and hang to dry over a clothesline. A wet camping trip will result in a gross tent—don't wait until your next trip to sort it out.

Store all camping equipment together and in an easily accessible location—so when the sun starts to shine you're ready to go.

Wash any sleeping bags, wipe down mattresses or roll mats and give your camping pots and pans a good scrub as soon as you're back home.

Index

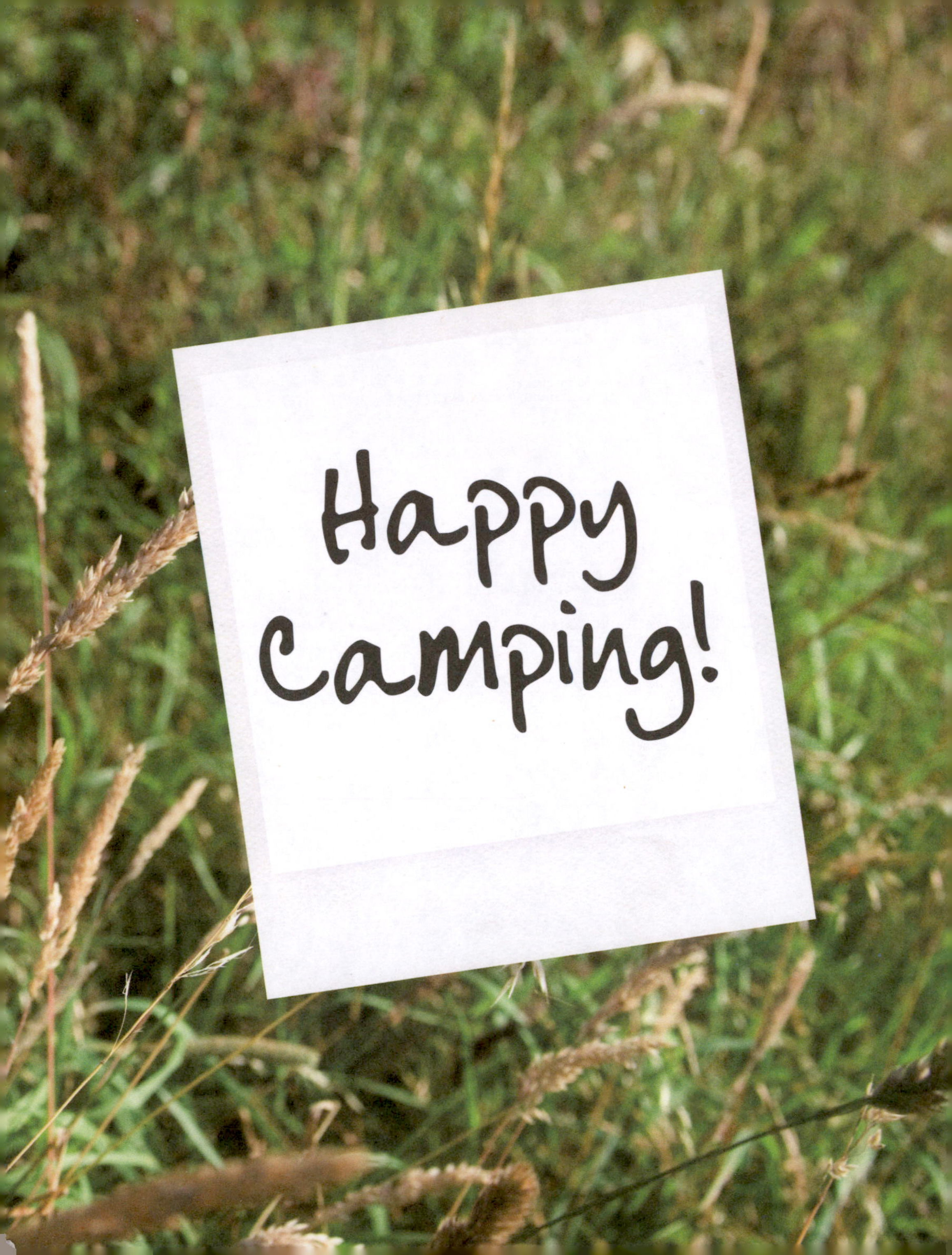
Happy
Camping!